YOUR KNOWLEDGE HAS VALUE

AF135859

- We will publish your bachelor's and master's thesis, essays and papers

- Your own eBook and book - sold worldwide in all relevant shops

- Earn money with each sale

Upload your text at www.GRIN.com
and publish for free

How the Counterinsurgency Strategies of Ethiopia, the United States and the AMISOM have Triggered the Growth of Al-Shabaab?

Gülşah Gürsoy

Bibliographic information published by the German National Library:

The German National Library lists this publication in the National Bibliography; detailed bibliographic data are available on the Internet at http://dnb.dnb.de.

ISBN: 9783346399694
This book is also available as an ebook.

© GRIN Publishing GmbH
Nymphenburger Straße 86
80636 München

Print and binding: Books on Demand GmbH, Norderstedt, Germany
Printed on acid-free paper from responsible sources.

The present work has been carefully prepared. Nevertheless, authors and publishers do not incur liability for the correctness of information, notes, links and advice as well as any printing errors.

GRIN web shop: https://www.grin.com/document/1010487

How the Counterinsurgency Strategies of Ethiopia, the United States and the AMISOM Have Triggered the Growth of Al-Shabaab?

- **Introduction**
- **Background:**
  - Somalia After Independence, 1969 Coup d'état and Ziad Barre Regime
  - Fall of Barre Regime, Civil War, Somaliland's Declaration of Independence, Islamic Courts Union (ICU), Ethiopian Invasions, Transitional Governments, Al-Shabaab, AMISOM
- **Lessons Learned from AMISOM**
- **Conclusion**
- **Bibliography**

Gülşah Gürsoy

Peace and Conflict Studies Master Program

Philipps Marburg University, Germany

11.09.2019

Introduction

Somali/Somalia is considered as a "failed state" by the international community, for it does not have functioning state institutions since the fall of Siad Barre regime in 1991. The constant political and humanitarian crises in Somalia have deeper roots in history (Hesse, 2015).

The territories where Somali people lived were colonized by French (north, today's Djibouti), British (today's Somaliland) and Italian (southern parts of today's Somali) states. While the imperial powers shared lands in Africa in 18th and 19th centuries, none of them considered exactly what is happening on the soil and which ethnic groups were living where. The borders that were drawn on maps have created enormous problems in the future that no one would ever imagined before. The different agendas and interests of imperial states have initiated conflicts among tribes (or clans), such as British was involved in extracting resources, while Italians were improving cultivation in southern parts. These different kinds of exploitation by imperial powers caused disputes about land and water resources among Somali clans (Thomas, 2016).

One of the astounding examples of land dispute in the region is Ogaden, which comprises ethnic Somali and Muslim population. The conflict over Ogaden can be traced back until the mid-19th century, when Ethiopia adjected it into its territory. Afterwards Ogaden passed in other hands between Somali and Ethiopia several times under colonial administrations of Italy and Britain and caused a war between Somali and Ethiopia in 1977-78. Today Ogaden officially belongs to Ethiopia, however, there is insurgency movements and unrest among people in the region (Bamfo, 2010).

Gaining independence from the colonial powers in 1st July 1960 did not give Somali a brighter future. Following democratic elections in 1964, 1967 and 1969, the country has witnessed a military coup in October 1969, which allowed Siad Barre to govern Somali until 1991 (Ingiriis, 2017). The fall of Barre regime has created a power vacuum, which was tried to be filled by several armed groups.

The power struggle between non-state actors in Somali was not left alone by foreign actors, such as the United States and Ethiopia. Among many others, the actions of these two states paved the way for the incredible growth of one of today's most dangerous and deadliest terrorist groups, Al-Shabaab. The group claims that they are fighting against foreign invaders in their country and they aim to establish an Islamic state (Hussein, 2017).

In the following chapters of this essay; the background of the insurgencies in Somali, counterinsurgency (COIN) responses from Ethiopia and the United States, and the reaction of insurgents will be summarized.

Background:

- **Somalia After Independence, 1969 Coup d'état and Siad Barre Regime**

Somalian state had many structural problems after gaining independence from colonial powers (British in the north and Italian in the south) and unification of post-colonial north and south. The systems such as education, taxation, governing, trainings in the military were all different than each other in the north and south, one in British style and the other Italian. Somalia tried to merge these two systems and eliminate the discrepancies between the regions; however, it did not work well as thought (Dualeh, 1994). There were many politicians from both regions who opposed the unification of two counties because of this huge divergency. Also, the majority and the influence in politics were in the hands of southern, which created opposition in the north against united Somalia. Doraad and Hawiye clans from south were the dominant groups in power between 1960 and 1969. The clan culture and structure are quite powerful and effective in Somalia, although politicians and religious authorities have tried to create more powerful Islamic identity among all Somalis and dissolve all clan-based discriminations and problems, it has never really worked (Ndegwa, 2018). Northern clans felt left out after the unification, and they were losing money and resources because of the structural changes made in favor of southern people; such as the changes in taxation system (Dualeh, 1994).

In the 60s after independence, Somalia had two parliamentary elections, respectively in 1964 and 1969, and between those they had presidential elections in 1967. Abdirashid Sharmake was elected as president, however, he could only serve two years as president since he was assassinated on 15th October 1969 by one of his guards. Right after Sharmake's funeral, the military took control of the administration in the country. The military regime, under Siad Barre's control, has abolished the government, the constitution and supreme court, banned the political parties (Hussein, 2017).

3

Sharmake's assassination was never thoroughly investigated. Since the government of Somalia had close ties with the West until 1969 and afterwards Barre regime had embraced socialism as a mere ideology of Somalian state, conspiracies about Sharmake's death were mainly as follows: attack was planned and realized by support of Soviet Union (Ingiriis, 2017). One of the incidents that can work for these conspiracies would be that the military got fully armed and alarmed after president's death, which would be in normal circumstances impossible because the Somalian army had to lock up their arms every night until they get orders from generals. Basically, after the funeral of president, Barre and his comrades did not have to find ways to arm the soldiers and make the coup, the army was already armed and ready, and this made it easier for top generals in the army to declare the military government (Dualeh, 1994).

Barre's regime did not bring answers to clan-based problems in Somalia, such as nepotism, many issues got even worse under his control. He appointed many of his friends and family members to top positions in government offices. Other than nepotism, Barre's regime was one of the clear examples of dictatorships in Africa. He oppressed all kinds of opposition, especially the ones from religious groups. During the first years of Barre's presidency, he was supported by Soviet Union and trying to imply "scientific socialism" in Somalia. It was called scientific because the dominating religion in Somalia was (and still is) Islam, which was not very compatible with socialism. As Barre embraced socialist ideas, he continued to act in many ways against it (nepotism was criticized by his allies in Soviets) and worsened clan-based discrimination in Somalia (Dualeh, 1994). Also, several Islamist groups were opposed to him and criticizing his government, defending Islamic rule and traditions to solve country's problems. At that time, these ideas were supported among Arab world. Because of severe oppression, arrests and execution of some Islamic leaders in Somalia, many of those groups started to continue their activities obscurely (Ndegwa, 2018).

Siad Barre was trained militarily under the fascist Italian commanders before Somali's independence. This is considered as one of the factors that made Barre very despotic (Dualeh, 1994). He wanted to pursue the idea of "Greater Somalia" during his presidency, which aims to bring all ethnic Somalis under one flag (including Ogaden region in Ethiopia). Although Ethiopia was also an ally of Soviet's, Barre did not abstain invading Ethiopian territory. Barre saw an opportunity in Ethiopia's weak situation and bad economy under military junta (between 1977-87 Ethiopia was governed by military regime) and wanted to be the man who annexed Ogaden to Somalian borders. So-called Ogaden War started in August 1977 with Somali's invasion in Ogaden (Jackson, 2010).

Somali troops were trained well under Soviet control; therefore, they could take control of Ogaden in 3 months. However, it was not what the big ally Soviets wanted, because initially the aim for Soviets in the west Africa region was establishment of a socialist states union to have control over this strategic region, also the oil sale to United States (Hussein, 2017). Therefore, the Union first tried to solve the problem by negotiations between two socialist states; Ethiopia and Somalia. Talks did not give positive results, but the Soviets did not want Ethiopia to lose territory. Because of that, the Soviet Union withdrew their support from Somalia and fully supported Ethiopian army, including bringing support troops from Yemen and Cuba (Hussein, 2017). This move pushed Somalian army back from Ogaden and forced Somalia to look for a new ally against Soviet Union: United States (Wood, 2018).

After Ogaden War and during the 1980s, the western aid to Somalia was in incredible amounts. The neoliberal policies of western states were implied in Somalia as well, to transfer it into a capitalist state, after its break-up with socialism. With the support of United States, World Bank and many other foreign aid organizations, some land reforms were made. For instance, they aimed to change the nomadic way of agriculture and register all farmers to some certain piece of land. These plans did not work well in Somalia and they ended up with corruption, exploitation of nomadic farmers and peasants, and unjust enrichment of urban elites and state officials (Besteman, 2017). The aid did not just help elites to get richer, it also helped the Barre regime to become even more autocratic and oppressive. The opposition was suppressed violently, especially in the northern regions of Somalia (Samatar, 1992).

The exclusion of any kind of opposition and impoverishment of people despite the tremendous rate of aid caused creation of armed opposition groups and separation movements within the Somali National Army. Some of these armed groups were Somali National Movement (SNM), Somali Salvation Democratic Front (SSDF), United Somali Congress (USC) and Somali Patriotic Movement (SPM) (Hussein, 2017). The defeat in the Ogaden War triggered the segregations within the army. Therefore, Barre increased the level of nepotism, he appointed people from his clan and some other clans that he can trust to high positions in the army. The vicious circle of people losing trust to government and Barre surrounding himself by an army of loyal clan members have made the state of Somalia just an "ostensible" one. Barre's regime started to lose control of some regions as early as 1988 and the country was already experiencing civil war (Robinson, 2016). By 1991, several armed groups were fighting over control of resources, many of them had arms but no military trainings and these clashes between armed tribes harmed Somalia a lot (Bamfo, 2010).

- ○ **Fall of Barre Regime, Civil War, Somaliland's Declaration of Independence, Islamic Courts Union (ICU), Ethiopian Invasions, Transitional Governments, Al-Shabaab, AMISOM**

In January 1991, the consolidation of several armed groups called United Somali Congress (USC) ousted Siad Barre regime in Mogadishu (these groups were obscurely supported by Ethiopian government) (Bamfo, 2010). However, ideals and plans of creating a peaceful Somalia after Barre were not easy to be realized. Right after unseating Barre and his comrades, the alliance of USC started to resolve. One of the leaders of armed groups, Ali Mahdi's self-declaration of "interim presidency" did not get approval by another strong leader; Aideed. Aideed and Ali Mahdi's groups were separated into two in their power struggle over Mogadishu respectively: Somali National Alliance (SNA) and Somali Salvation Alliance (SSA). Until 1993, some military interventions by United Nations (UNOSOM) and United States (UNITAF) took place to finish these clashes, however, they did not give positive results. In 1993, supporters of Aideed shot a US airplane and killed soldiers in it. After this event (infamously known as "Black Hawk Down"), both the United Nations and the United States withdrew all their troops from Somalia until 1995 (Ndegwa, 2018). The Al-Qaeda leader Osama Bin Laden then announced that he helped with the supplies used for this attack against US airplanes, which only aided to the understanding of Somalia as a nest for terror cells by upcoming US governments (Wood, 2018).

Among the conflicts between everyone who holds weapons, another group called Somali National Movement (SNM) in the north did not join the alliances with southern clans and declared their own independent state in May 1991: Somaliland. They did not get any international recognition. Similarly, in 1998, in the northwest of Somali, Puntland region has announced its local autonomy. Different than Somaliland, Puntland considered itself as a part of Somalian state, but they had as well their own local government (Thomas, 2016).

Another very important part of the puzzle in Somalian context are the Islamic groups. Since the 1980s, more than ten (known) Islamic groups (mostly armed) were founded in Somalia. By the time, depending on the course of events, some of them have created allies, some started to fight against each other. The main triggering factors for the born of these groups can be mentioned as: oppressive policies of Siad Barre against religious groups, bad economic situation, and the trend in Muslim and Arab world that suggests using Islamic principles to solve the social and economic problems in Muslim societies (Ndegwa, 2018).

One of the prominent Islamic groups in Somalia history is Al-Ittihad Al-Islamiya (AIAI), which was founded initially in 1984 (Stanford University, 2019). The group emerged from the attempts of organizing the society and solving disputes among people by the help of Islamic Courts. They implied Sharia Law in these courts, and they were mainly active in southern parts of the country. They have also aimed to unify Somali people under one flag by using Islam as uniting power instead of tribal motives (Hussein, 2017). However, after the fall of Barre, like many other armed groups, AIAI also started to get armed and enhance its control over regions. They allied with Ogaden National Liberation Front (ONLF), which is a separatist organization based in Ogaden region of Ethiopia, to support the ONLF in their anti-Ethiopian fight. AIAI carried out attacks in Ethiopia, especially to security points. Therefore, AIAI has become a threat for Ethiopia's security, and it caused Ethiopia's invasion in Somalia in 1997 to finish AIAI. After the attacks in Ethiopia, United States added AIAI in its "terrorist groups list" (Ndegwa, 2018).

Ethiopia's counterinsurgency strategy for Somalia, basically the 1997's military intervention and deactivating AIAI militias, did not bring an effective solution in the long term. The aim of Ethiopia was to stop the Islamic movements in its neighbor, Ethiopia was perceiving the Islam in Somalia as threatening because of its own Christian population. AIAI in Somalia was not functioning anymore after the Ethiopian invasion, but several groups have emerged from its remnants, such as Islamic Courts Union (ICU). This group arose from Sharia courts of AIAI, however, ICU's main interest in the beginning was protecting the interests of businesspeople and create stable and safe zones in Somalia. Different from AIAI, the ICU did not fight militarily against Ethiopia or other foreign powers in the beginning of its time. Business milieu needed ICU's support and security against warlords, since they did not want to pay taxes to several armed groups and they needed stability for their businesses (Ingiriis, 2017). With these aims,

7

the ICU was working as the enforcing body of Sharia law in Somalia. Nevertheless, by the time the ICU got politicized more than expected. According to some Somalis, ICU was doing good in terms of bringing stability and peace in Somalia, although it brought many restrictions on social life in line with Sharia law (Thomas, 2016).

Until 2000, there were several local and international attempts made to negotiate and build a state structure in Somalia, however, none of them were fruitful. The peace conference in Djibouti in 2000 was the first time that a government was founded in Mogadishu: "Transitional National Government" (TNG) (Robinson, 2016). This government was not effective and stable as it had three presidents in four years only and was just able to control some parts of Mogadishu. Because TNG did not receive enough recognition and support internally and externally, especially from neighboring Ethiopia and Kenya, it was eventually abolished (Thomas, 2016).

In 2004, the TNG was succeeded by another stabilization attempt, "Transitional Federal Government" (TFG), which was founded in city of Baidoa. TFG was an initiation of a regional organization, that was supported by the US and the European Union, which is called "Intergovernmental Authority on Trade and Development" (IGAD). IDAG was consisted of six countries in the region (Uganda, Kenya, Ethiopia, Sudan, Eritrea, Djibouti) (Bamfo, 2010). TFG also could not work efficiently in Somalia just like the previous governments, because of non-stop clan crashes and power struggles within the government (Robinson, 2016). In 2005, TFG government requested a military intervention by IGAD states to help carrying its head office to Mogadishu. However, this so-called IGAD peace building force for Somalia (IGASOM) was not deployed in the end because of lack of resources and unwillingness of IGAD states to send their soldiers to Somalia (E. Bruton & Williams, 2014). The idea of deployment of IGASOM mission was perceived by the ICU as another Western "invasion plan" as it was originated from the western-funded organization IGAD (Hussein, 2017).

It is also worth mentioning that TFG was working in line with Ethiopia's requests (Marchal, 2009). For many Somalians, the ICU was much more favorable than the TFG. Despite the strict Sharia law, ICU was able to provide peace and stability. No matter how "non-democratic" it was, many people in Somalia would prefer it rather than TFG because TFG represented the top-down "democratization" approach of Western powers. However, the ICU was consisted of their own people and working in line with religion and clan relations, which foreign invaders were not able to understand and deal with. One of the reasons why TFG was not able to fully function in Somalia was its lack of public support (Wood, 2018).

By 2006, Islamic Courts Union got much more powerful in terms of governance and they were against the existence of the TFG in Somalia. The ICU has forced the TFG to move its center from Mogadishu to Baidoa. And after that Mogadishu was under the control of the ICU. This event was perceived as a "growing Islamic threat" by the United States as well as the neighbor Ethiopia. Both did not want an Islamic state in the region, which seemed to them as the main aim of ICU (Farole, 2018).

In Somalia the Islamist extremism was never the biggest case before 2000s, although Saudis sponsored many madrasas (Islamic schools) and tried to spread Wahhabi ideology in Somalia in 90s. The effects of these schools were to be seen clearly for the first time in 2005, when small groups of militias started to attack the TFG and western people who live in Somalia. These attacks were the first steps of the extremist Islamic movement which was ready to be institutionalized in Somalia (E. Bruton & Williams, 2014).

The United States and Ethiopia were in favor of bringing the TFG back in Mogadishu again, instead of the ICU's Islamic Sharia governance in the capital. The sudden growth of ICU, attacks against non-Muslims and the "statelessness" (in terms of modern understanding) in Somalia terrified the United States administration, as Somalia could be the new safe spot for Al-Qaeda terrorists who run away from the Middle East. Also, the United States' post 9/11 war on terror strategy was requiring an action in the horn of Africa since Al-Qaeda members were going there. Everything which is somehow related to Al-Qaeda must have been destroyed, according to the US strategy. So, the US existence in Somalia was in those years aiming to catch the Al-Qaeda members. Therefore, Ethiopia invaded Somalia in December 2006, to isolate the ICU and bring the TFG from Baidoa back to the capital Mogadishu. This invasion was motivated and financially backed by the United States, although officially the US officials rejected the claims about it (Bamfo, 2010).

Beside using Ethiopia as a tool in the region to foster the so-called "democratic state building" in Somalia, the United States had very complex and conflicting counterinsurgency strategy in 2006. The government had different approaches on their table (there were differences between the plans of CIA -US Central Intelligence Agency- and State Department, both offered different strategies). Instead of State Department's negotiation and mitigation strategy, the government chose the CIA's way, which was to fund some local militias in Somalia and try to capture the Al-Qaeda leaders in the country by these militias' help. However, it did not work out as they had planned. This strategy only helped to create bigger opposition against foreign intervention in Somalia and provided arms to many untrained normal people and caused them to turn into unorganized armed militias. (Wood, 2018).

Ethiopia's US-backed invasion in Somalia ended in the beginning of 2009, which took much longer than initially planned. By the time Ethiopian forces have defeated the ICU militarily in Mogadishu, however, they were not able to exterminate it. To the opposite, some new groups have been founded already in 2007 from ICU's leftovers: Re-liberation of Somalia (ARS) and Al-Shabaab (meaning: The Youth) The defeat of ICU in Mogadishu created a power vacuum and rivalry between armed militia groups, to gain the control of Mogadishu (Ndegwa, 2018). Ethiopia's initial aim to bring the TFG to Mogadishu and finish the ICU completely, did not work. Instead, these three yearlong interventions radicalized extremist ICU members even more and motivated them to defend their religion and country against infidels. This event is considered as the root cause of Al-Shabaab jihadist movement's born in Somalia (Anderson, 2014).

ICU itself as a group was not considered as extremist, however, after its fall, some extremist members of it were gathered under the name of Al-Shabaab. This new group was consisted of more radical Islamists than any other militia group in Somalia. Ethiopia's Christian population was as a justification for their case and fight, because to them Ethiopia was as foreign and Christian as other invaders (Wood, 2018).

During Ethiopian invasion (2006-2009), because of international pressure the United Nations Security Council and the African Union have decided to deploy an African Union Mission to Somalia (later will be called as AMISOM). This idea was derived from the fact that Ethiopian existence did not have any positive effects in Somalia, quite the contrary it was just radicalizing the militias there and increasing the hatred against Ethiopians in their neighboring country (Anderson, 2014). Sending African troops to protect the TFG from terrorist groups was kind of a "local solution" for the constant governance problems in Somalia. AMISOM was supposed to train Somali's army -or re-create it-, protect the infrastructure, support the humanitarian organizations to deliver their help to people in need, and promote reconciliation attempts between TFG and armed groups (Bamfo, 2010). Since many African states were not willing to send their troops to Somalia, AMISOM mission was delayed several times. Therefore, Ethiopian invasion continued until 2009, because there were no other troops to replace them and both Ethiopia and the West did not let Somalia stay without foreign intervention which is fighting against Somalian militias. Ethiopian troops were not careful about civilians, which caused many civilian killings in Somalia. Foreign military involvement radicalized thousands of people in Somalia, since according to many Somalis foreigners were only killing Somalian people and worsening the situation in their country. In the end even many people who were not actively fighting amongst insurgents, were supporting the idea of defending their country against foreigners. (Anderson, 2014).

Al-Shabaab was recruiting especially young Somalis by its effective campaign against foreign and non-Muslim troops' existence in their country. Already in 2007, they organized several bomb attacks and targeted Ethiopian military bases in Somalia and killed many soldiers. Ethiopian army's response was not merciful, they used phosphorus bombs and killed Somalian civilians. These incidents only helped the Al-Shabaab to gain more support in the public's eyes. In couple of months Al-Shabaab was controlling some regions of Mogadishu and harming the Ethiopian army heavily. Therefore, Ethiopia deployed more troops to Somalia (E. Bruton & Williams, 2014). While intervening heavily in Somalia, Ethiopia did not have very good circumstances at home. Its population has suffered from poverty and lack of freedom of protest and expression. Ethiopian government was criticized because they did not focus on their own people's urgent problems and they were oppressing the opposition in their homeland, at the same time they were trying to "fix things" in Somalia (Bamfo, 2010). When Ethiopia left Somalia in 2009, the humanitarian situation was terrible in the country. 1.3 million people were internally displaced, and more than 3 million people needed urgent humanitarian aid. These numbers alone show the uselessness foreign military invasion in Somalia (Anderson, 2014).

United States added Al-Shabaab to its terrorist organizations list in 2008, which created the legal base for the US army to intervene directly in Somalia. Al-Shabaab was criticized by western media as a terrorist organization, mainly because of its opposition to western-supported TGF. Although Al-Shabaab derived from Somalia itself, it was pictured in western world as a threat to the country and was put on the target list of the west, mainly the USA.

The US air-strikes and military intervention did not do nothing but radicalizing and empowering the Al-Shabaab as the "main defender" of anti-Western Islamic movement in Somalia. (Besteman, 2017). The idea of "good Islam" which was advocated by Western powers and Ethiopia, was not good enough to convince Somali people to be against radical jihadists, because it was perceived by Somalis as the "American version of Islam" (Marchal, 2009).

AMISOM faced many difficulties in Somalia especially in its first years. As it was a "peace-keeping mission", it was only allowed to defend itself and the locations under its supervision (such as airports). AMISOM was not fighting against Al-Shabaab actively and offensively, like Ethiopian or USA troops did before. It was a difficult mission to operate as peace did not exist in Somalia that time, which a peace-keeping operation could help to maintain (Ndegwa, 2018).

After Ethiopian forces left Somalia in 2009, AMISOM's responsibility increased and the pressure on the mission got bigger (UNSC, 2009). It was the only "legitimate" troop in Somalia to fight against the insurgency and gain control of Mogadishu and surroundings, create a safe environment for the TFG to work. Despite the challenges, TFG was settled in Mogadishu again with the help of AMISOM (Jones, Liepman, & Chandler, 2016).

Al-Shabaab was enhancing its capacity and public support during the time AMISOM got better organized and improved its mission in Somalia. Al-Shabaab did campaigning for its purposes, it turned itself into an "jihadi insurgency movement" from just a small terrorist organization. The movement was Islamist and nationalist at the same time, trying to impress different society groups. They have defended the idea that Somalia was under constant occupation by foreign troops (including AMISOM) and Christians, and as Muslim Somalis they must defend their country and save it from foreigners. Another important point of their campaign was the unification of all Somali people under one flag. Al-Shabaab could find support from some previous ICU and AIAI members, and therefore could extend its control amongst regions which for example Hawiye and Rahanweyn clans lived in. Clan relations and dialogue were very important to build interpersonal relations for the group to get "allowance" to move freely in many regions. Al-Shabaab attacks were mainly targeting the military or government offices, however, many civilians were killed by the attacks as well. The terrorist attacks carried by Al-Shabaab militants aimed to show that they have the capacity to harm and defeat the government and Somalian army (Ndegwa, 2018).

In 2010, Al-Shabaab organized bombing attacks in Uganda and killed 76 people. After this incident, by the decision of UN Security Council, the mission of AMISOM was updated. The AMISOM was now a "peace-enforcement" mission and had right to carry military operations against Al-Shabaab (UNSC, 2009).

In 2010 and 2011, AMISOM troops attacked Al-Shabaab in Mogadishu to take the city under government's control. Finally, after the battles in 2011, they were able to control most of the city (Wood, 2018). The way that Al-Shabaab got control over so many regions in Mogadishu was not only fighting, instead they were negotiating with clan leaders and getting support from them, which gave them an upper hand against the AMISOM and government. This also shows that many clan leaders and Somalis believed in Al-Shabaab rather than AMISOM and cooperated with the insurgent group (Ndegwa, 2018).

The change in AMISOM's strategy after 2009 had three major points: decapitation (means killing the most important leaders of terrorist group), liberation of cities (gaining control of important centers such as Mogadishu) and increasing the troops' strength (UNSC, 2009). The strategy change helped AMISOM and TFG to gain more control over larger territories in Somalia, however, it did not eradicate Al-Shabaab fully. The group continued its attacks by changing tactics constantly, such as organizing suicide bombings in neighboring countries, enlarging its capacity in rural and remote areas etc. Al-Shabaab conducted several bombings in many neighboring countries because those countries were contributing AMISOM by sending troops and providing military training to Somali's national armed forces (Jones, Liepman, & Chandler, 2016).

Only in 2011, the AMISOM and TFG were able to control the capital Mogadishu fully. Following that in 2012, Transitional Federal government was abolished, and elections were held in Somalia. New Federal Government was founded, and the country is since then in a "post-transitional" phase (Ononogbu & Nwangwu, 2018).

Between 2012 and 2016, AMISOM continued its fight against Al-Shabaab with the same counterinsurgency tactics as mentioned above (the three points). However, these years were also the most violent years of Al-Shabaab (Wood, 2018). The group killed more than 5000 people only in between those years and most of the fatalities were civilians, including many government officials (Ndegwa, 2018). The group announced its allegiance with Al-Qaeda in

2012, which shows their efforts to find more support from international jihadist movement and continue fighting against the Somali government and AMISOM (Ononogbu & Nwangwu, 2018).

AMISOM did not get fully support from Somali people, despite its "African" troops it was still a foreign intervenor in the eyes of Somalis. Another reason for AMISOM's unpopularity is the damage it caused during the fights with Al-Shabaab. The mission was focused on defending the TFG and eliminating Al-Shabaab, the fighting areas especially in Mogadishu turned into real warzones and many people had to leave the town. The mission disregarded the humanitarian crises and the people in urgent need, which caused them loss of legitimacy in the hearts of Somalis. As May 2017, around 6.7 million people in Somalia need urgent humanitarian aid. The relevant stable government and weakening Al-Shabaab militarily does not improve the lives of people in the country (Ononogbu & Nwangwu, 2018).

Al-Shabaab have lost lots of territories, public support and members in recent years, however, it continues its attacks. They have changed structurally from an insurgency movement which acts like a legitimate governing body, back to a terrorist organization which depends on terrorist tactics and controls very small areas (Jones, Liepman, & Chandler, 2016).

o **Lessons Learned from AMISOM**

AMISOM could not fully reach its aims in Somalia because of several reasons. First, there was never a good and internationally agreed COIN strategy about Somalia. The international actors who were trying to impose a type of political regime in the war-torn country, did not know enough about the local clan relations and the whole Somali context. This lack of knowledge brought bad intervention strategies. Although they were planned by "COIN experts", they did not fit the country (E. Bruton & Williams, 2014).

What AMISOM and other interventions tried to achieve in Somalia was technically bringing an unelected government into force without the consent of its own people (Hussein, 2017). Even though Somali people were not hundred percent happy in the areas that Al-Shabaab controlled, they collaborated most of the time with the insurgents and accepted the way Al-Shabaab govern their areas. For many Somalis in southern regions, TFG and AMISOM were just foreign powers who increase the level of fighting in Somalia, on the other hand the Al-Shabaab was a local power and it was providing some humanitarian services to its people and got tolerated by the public (Ononogbu & Nwangwu, 2018). The only time the AMISOM started to get public support was when Al-Shabaab did some mistakes such as hindering the humanitarian aid when people were in urgent need during famine (E. Bruton & Williams, 2014).

There were also technical deficiencies that AMISOM struggled from, for instance the lack of support from contributing countries. The troops were always deployed later than they should have, and the numbers were not enough as planned. The political leadership of African Union (AU) was not good and strong enough to coordinate a successful operation under AMISOM, there was always conflict of interest between member states such as Kenya and Ethiopia (Farole, 2018). The political debates in AU left AMISOM alone on its feet while it was trying to gain some leverage against Al-Shabaab. (E. Bruton & Williams, 2014).

AMISOM's struggles were also about the power of Al-Shabaab. The insurgency has controlled many economic resources, which gave them power over territories. Combined with the support from some clans, the physical power made Al-Shabaab even harder to destroy. AMISOM's local partner TFG was not able to provide the same power to the mission since the TFG itself did not have legitimacy amongst public. The bad and "foreign invader" image of AMISOM got even worse by time because they did not pay attention to civil population and caused many civilians' deaths (E. Bruton & Williams, 2014).

Conclusion

Somalia's history is full of grievances and problems, which were never truly understood and addressed by the powers who tried to "help" Somalia. Starting from colonial administrations' time, foreign interventions have given more negative results than positive.

After the independence, the country has witnessed to the scrambles of cold-war, dictatorship, oppression and the resistance. It was never left alone with its problems, there was always foreign actors playing different roles in Somalia.

The most recent and ongoing problem of Somalia is the power struggle between the Federal Government and military groups, mainly Al-Shabaab. The insurgency which grew up by this Islamist jihadist group is mainly the result of Ethiopian invasion in 2006-2009. Demolition of ICU in Mogadishu gave the chance to Al-Shabaab to come to light and fill the gap of "Somalian governance". Because the ICU was "Islamist", Ethiopia and the United States have created the legal grounds for their suspicions against ICU and defined it as terrorist threat. The aim of Western states to create a "liberal democracy" in Somalia did not work out as in many other examples such as Iraq. As a reaction to foreign involvement, Somalian people supported Al-Shabaab's growth. Since the group found some sort of legitimacy in its people's eyes, despite the damage they gave to Somalia, it is still hard to wipe them out.

Bibliography

Anderson, N. (2014). Peacekeepers Fighting a Counterinsurgency Campaign: A Net Assessment of the African Union Mission in Somalia. *Studies in Conflict & Terrorism*.

Bamfo, N. A. (2010). Ethiopia's invasion of Somalia in 2006: Motives and Lessons Learned. *African Journal of Political Science and International Relations*, 55-65.

Besteman, C. (2017). Experimenting in Somalia: The New Security Empire. *SAGE Journals*, 404-420.

Dualeh, H. A. (1994). *From Barre to Aideed, Somalia: The Agony of a Nation.* Nairobi: Stellagraphics Ltd.

E. Bruton, B., & Williams, P. D. (2014). *Counterinsurgency in Somalia: Lessons Learned from the African Union Mission in Somalia 2007-2013.* Joint Special Operations University.

Farole, S. A. (2018). Regional security institutions and weak states: The case of post-conflict Somalia and the Inter-Governmental Authority on Development (IGAD). *Comparative Strategy*, 472-484.

General, U. S. (2009). *Secretary-General's Reports Submitted to the Security Council in 2009.* Retrieved from United Nations Security Council: https://undocs.org/S/2009/503

Hesse, B. J. (2015). Why Deploy to Somalia? Understanding Six African Countries' Reasons for Sending Soldiers to One of the World's Most Failed States. *The Journal of the Middle East and Africa*, 329-352.

Hussein, A. L. (2017). RELATIONSHIP BETWEEN FOREIGN INTERVENTION AND TERRORISM: A CASE STUDY OF ETHIOPIA`S MILITARY INTERVENTION IN SOMALIA. *A Thesis Submitted to the School of Arts & Sciences in Partial Fulfillment of the Requirement for the Degree of Master of Arts in International Relations*. Nairobi, Kenya: UNITED STATES INTERNATIONAL UNIVERSITY-AFRICA.

Ingiriis, M. H. (2017). Who Assassinated the Somali President in October 1969? The Cold War, the Clan Connection, or the Coup d'État. *African Security*, 131-154.

Jackson, D. R. (2010). The Ogaden War and the Demise of Détente. *SAGE Journals*, 26-40.

Jones, Liepman, & Chandler. (2016). *Counterterrorism and Counterinsurgency in Somalia Assessing the Campaign Against Al Shabaab.* Santa Monica, California: the RAND Corporation.

Marchal, R. (2009). A tentative assessment of the Somali Harakat Al-Shabaab. *Journal of Eastern African Studies*, 381-404.

Nations, U. (2012, February). *UN MEETINGS COVERAGE AND PRESS RELEASES*. Retrieved from https://www.un.org/press/en/2012/sc10550.doc.htm

Ndegwa, L. W. (2018). An analysis of the counterterrorism (CT) and counterinsurgency (COIN) operations employed by African Union Mission in Somalia (AMISOM) to counter the threat of al-Shabaab in Somalia (2007- 2016). Cape Town, South Africa: University of Cape Town.

Ononogbu, & Nwangwu. (2018). Counter-Insurgency Operations of the African Union and Mitigation of Humanitarian Crisis in Somalia. *Mediterranean Journal of Social Sciences*, 117-129.

Robinson, C. (2016). Revisiting the rise and fall of the Somali Armed Forces. *Defense & Security Analysis*, 237-252.

Samatar, A. I. (1992). Destruction of State and Society in Somalia: Beyond the Tribal Convention. *The Journal of Modem African Studies*, 625-641.

Stanford University, C. f. (2019). *Mapping Militants Project*. Retrieved from https://cisac.fsi.stanford.edu/mappingmilitants

Thomas, S. (2016). *Somalia Challenges and Opportunities in Peacebuilding*. Columbus, Ohio: Center for Policy Analysis & Research (CfPAR).

UNSC. (2009). *United Nations Security Council*. Retrieved from https://www.un.org/securitycouncil/content/secretary-generals-reports-submitted-security-council-2009

Wood, M. (2018). Contemporary U.S. Counter-terrorism Strategy toward Somalia. Cape Town, South Africa: University of Cape Town.